"The earnest seeker and hopeful discoverer...walks through the densest crowd uninterrupted, and, as it were, in a straight line."

Henry David Thoreau

Fussy-cut

MARINER'S COMPASS

Ann S. Lainhart

Dedication

This book is dedicated to my mother, Catherine B. Lainhart, who loved to sew, and to my father, William S. Lainhart, who loved to knit. Their support and their genes were essential in my pursuing an interest in hand work, especially quilting.

Located in Paducah, Kentucky, the American Quilter's Society (AQS) is dedicated to promoting the accomplishments of today's quilters. Through its publications and events, AQS strives to honor today's quiltmakers and their work and to inspire future creativity and innovation in quiltmaking.

Executive Book Editor: Andi Reynolds
Editor: Vivian Ritter
Graphic Design: Lynda Smith
Cover Design: Michael Buckingham
Photography: Charles R. Lynch

Additional copies of this book may be ordered from the American Quilter's Society, PO Box 3290, Paducah, KY 42002-3290, or online at www.AmericanQuilter.com.

Library of Congress Cataloging-in-Publication Data

Lainhart, Ann S.
  Fussy-cut mariner's compass / by Ann S. Lainhart.
    p. cm.
  ISBN 978-1-57432-975-9
  1. Patchwork--Patterns. 2. Quilting--Patterns. 3. Stars in art. I. Title.

TT835.L27 2009
746.46'041--dc22

2008051067

American Quilter's Society
P. O. Box 3290 • Paducah, KY 42002-3290
www.AmericanQuilter.com

Proudly printed and bound in the United States of America

Contents

Fussy-cut Mariner's Compass © Ann S. Lainhart

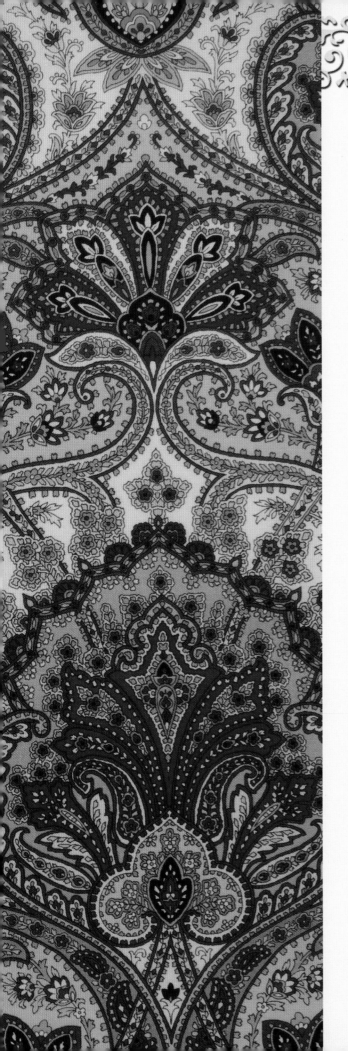

Preface

During the summers from 1994 to 2002 I owned The Quilted Gallery in Rocky Neck Art Colony in Gloucester, Massachusetts. My gallery included a studio with three large windows overlooking Smith Cove—my little piece of heaven. Being able to quilt for five months of the year took my quilting in directions I might not have gone otherwise. Exploring fussy-cutting was one of those paths.

I love designs that play with the eye and that is what first drew me to traditional Mariner's Compass blocks. The three-dimensional effect of what look like layers of points is wonderful. From the time I made my first Compass with points fussy-cut from a symmetrically patterned fabric, I became intrigued with the possibilities.

In the last few years, fabrics with symmetrical designs have become increasingly available, making it easy to find just the right designs for fussy-cutting. Each Compass that I make is in some ways a surprise to me. Even though I now have a good idea of what fabrics will work well when fussy-cut, I still enjoy seeing the complete design for the first time after sewing the final seam and opening the center.

While the Mariner's Compass is not an easy block to construct, because all the steps need to be done carefully and accurately, I think most quilters will enjoy the challenge when the results make such wonderful and dramatic designs.

A large fussy-cut Compass can make a perfect center for a medallion quilt. Several Compasses with different designs cut from the same symmetrical fabric can be used together in one quilt. Just one fussy-cut Compass can make a very nice small quilted wallhanging, or it can be mounted or matted to make a lovely piece of framed art.

I hope this book will inspire you to make at least one fussy-cut Mariner's Compass.

Fussy-cut Mariner's Compass © Ann S. Lainhart

Choosing Fabric for Fussy-cut Mariner's Compasses

Fig. 1. This stunning block is the result of fussy-cutting the fabrics to achieve the Kaleidoscope effect.

Ann S. Lainhart ✿ Fussy-cut Mariner's Compass

Today's quiltmakers are incredibly fortunate to enjoy a wealth of fabric choices. Never before has there been such a variety to satisfy every quilter's tastes and needs. Choosing just the right print for your Mariner's Compass block is part of the challenge—and certainly part of the fun.

What Is Fussy-cutting?

"Fussy-cutting" refers to isolating a fabric motif and cutting patches exactly alike. The deliberate placement of the patches within the block produces a kaleidoscopic effect (Fig. 1, page 9). Although the term has come into popular use in the last couple of decades, the process of fussy-cutting fabrics has been around for generations. Many antique quilts illustrate this technique. The next time you see a Grandmother's Flower Garden quilt made in the 1930s, check out the fabric placement. You may find fussy-cut patches.

With this fussy-cutting method, you carefully select the design specifically for the Compass so that the fabric print matches along seam lines between patches. Each patch is cut individually. This method produces the intricate designs you see in these Compasses.

Master quilters such as Jinny Beyer and Paula Nadelstern have made quilts with fussy-cut fabrics for years, and they both design fabric lines specifically for precision cutting. Many fabric manufacturers are now producing prints that appeal to fussy-cutters. Your dilemma won't be finding a print that's suitable for this technique—it will be choosing which one to experiment with first.

I began fussy-cutting in the mid-1970s using border prints to enhance traditional blocks such as Eight-Pointed Star, Kaleidoscope, and Card Trick. I first heard the term fussy-cutting on one of Eleanor Burns's television programs. She was isolating and cutting a particular flower for the center square of the block she was making. I realized that fussy-cutting was what I had been doing for years. The first time that I fussy-cut a Mariner's Compass block with eight points coming together in the center, I was off and running making fussy-cut Compasses.

Which Fabric Designs Work Best?

Fabric that is appropriate for a fussy-cut Mariner's Compass must have a symmetrical design; that is, the printed motifs need to reflect one another in mirror image on each side of a center line. This line can be real or it may be seen only in your mind's eye.

Some fabrics have a multitude of motifs that are symmetrical while other fabrics have just a few. Some prints may be too small-scale to be very effective.

Look for prints with good contrast between the elements of the design so the kaleidoscope effect in the center stands out well. As you read this chapter and examine the blocks and fabrics, you will become more familiar with the kinds of prints to look for.

The template for the eight primary point patches of a Compass block is kite-shaped (Fig. 2). The template is aligned on the fabric so that its center bisects the motif and the same print is on both sides of the shape. The eight patches are cut exactly alike and, once they are joined, the design flows from one patch to the next (Fig. 3).

Fig. 2 and Fig. 3. The kite-shaped template placement on the fabric in figure 2 yields the result in the Compass block in Figure 3.

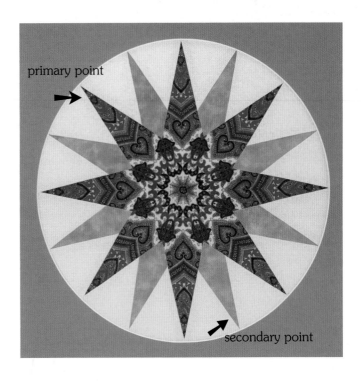

primary point

secondary point

Fig. 4. Look closely to see both symmetrical and asymmetrical designs in this fabric.

Look for fabric that is printed with some symmetrical designs that repeat, like the one in figure 4. The central patches must be fussy-cut to obtain the kaleidoscopic effect. The other points of the Compass can be fussy-cut too, although they can be cut from coordinating, nonsymmetrical fabrics.

Most useful is fabric with some large-scale symmetrical motifs that fit nicely within each individual patch (Fig. 5, page 13). It could be distracting to have part of one motif at the center point and part of an adjacent motif at the outer point of the patch, although that may be just what you want if the design works.

Fig. 5. Large-scale prints with nearly symmetrical motifs like the one shown here work best.

Much of the delight with fussy-cutting comes in discovering the potential of your chosen material. Look at the fabric shown here and then at the three blocks with the varying centers to get an idea of the possibilities from one print.

Fig. 6. One elaborate print can produce a variety of Kaleidoscopic designs.

Fig. 7. The look from the top template in figure 6

Fig. 8. The look from the central template in figure 6

Fig. 9. The look from the bottom template in figure 6

Fig. 10. It is the band of white on the primary points that allows enough contrast with the secondary points in this block.

The kaleidoscopic design in the center of the Mariner's Compass changes dramatically when the primary points are cut from a different area of the fabric. The results can be surprising (refer to pages 14–15). See the quilt FLORENTINE COMPASSES on page 71 in which each block is cut from different parts of the same fabric.

The secondary points of a Mariner's Compass—the eight points that are behind the primary points—can also be fussy-cut from a different section of the same fabric. When both sets of points are cut from the same material, be certain that the primary points are different enough in value and design so that they stand out from the secondary points (Fig. 10).

Fig. 11.

Fig. 12.

tertiary point

secondary point

Fig. 13. The fabrics in figures 11 and 12 contrast enough to yield these interesting secondary and tertiary points.

There are undoubtedly other prints in a fabric line that will go well with the fabric chosen for the primary points. In the block in figure 13, two fabrics from the same line (Figs. 11–12, page 17) are fussy-cut for the secondary and tertiary points, the 16 points that appear at the back of the Compass. The fabrics coordinate nicely in color and imagery, but they are different enough so that the three sets of points are distinct (Fig. 13).

Of course, any fabrics that work well with the primary print can be used for other parts of the block. In figure 14 on page 19, snowflakes from a second fabric line are fussy-cut for the secondary points.

Note that in the blocks already shown, the triangular patches between the points are made with light solid or tone-on-tone fabrics so that the round outline of the Compass stands out against the surrounding background square. By using the same fabric for the triangular patches and the background square, the round outline vanishes and the Compass appears to be floating (Fig. 15).

Not every motif will be as successful as another. At first, your selections may be by trial and error as you seek the most interesting designs. But the more that you experiment with fussy-cutting, the better you will become at choosing the patterns that are most likely to produce lovely blocks. More about choosing and auditioning fabric is found in chapter two.

Fig. 14. The fussy-cut snowflake print is used in the secondary points for an additional design element.

Fig. 15. Using the same fabric for background triangles in the Compass and in the background square makes the design appear to float.

Fig. 16. Motifs spaced closely together require less yardage to obtain the number of desired repeats.

How Much Fabric Does It Take?

Yardage for a fussy-cut Mariner's Compass depends on the size of the block, the number of repeat motifs from selvage to selvage (width of fabric), and the distance between the repeats along the length of the fabric.

In the figure 16 fabric, the motifs are closely spaced from selvage to selvage and the distance between the repeats is relatively short, so one yard of fabric should be enough for the eight primary points.

The figure 17 print on page 21 has only two or three motifs from selvage to selvage—depending on the motif chosen—and a repeat distance of 18". Approximately two yards would be needed to cut the eight primary points.

To be certain that you purchase enough fabric for your planned project, take the templates for the primary points (see pages 38–39) to the fabric store. Open up the yardage, identify a likely design, and count the number of repeats across the width and

Fig. 17. Larger or wider motifs require more yardage to obtain enough repeats.

down the length. Remember that you'll need eight points all alike. Buy enough fabric to have a couple of extra motifs in case a cutting mistake is made.

For a 12" Mariner's Compass, ¼ yard each is needed for the secondary points and for the triangular background patches between the points. The square in which the Compass is set is 16", so a fat quarter (18" x 22") is needed. If the background square is cut from the same fabric as either the secondary points or triangular pieces, ½ yard of that fabric is needed. Be sure to cut this ½ yard down the fold so a fat quarter is preserved for the background square.

For an 18" Mariner's Compass, ¼ yard each is needed for the secondary points, the tertiary points, and the triangular patches between the points. The background square in which the Compass is set is 22", so ¾ yard is needed. If the background fabric is the same used to cut the secondary points, the tertiary points, or the triangular patches, one yard

Fig. 18. If using the same fabric for points and background square, cut out the square first.

is required. Cut the background square and set it aside before cutting any other patches from this fabric (Fig. 18).

For a 30" Mariner's Compass, ½ yard each is needed for the secondary points, the tertiary points, and the triangular patches between the points. The background square in which the Compass is set is 34" to 36", so one yard is necessary.

If the secondary or tertiary points are also fussy-cut,

then the amount of fabric will depend on the number of motifs from selvage to selvage and the distance between the repeats along the length of the fabric. Take the templates to the fabric store, lay them on the material on the likely motifs, and count the repeats to determine the amount to purchase.

If you plan to use the same fabric for more than one set of points, the amount of yardage will be determined by the location of the chosen motifs. It might be possible to cut the secondary and tertiary

Fig. 19. The background is cut from the same fabric as the triangular pieces

points from yardage left over between the cuts for the primary points. More about cutting patches is in chapter two.

If the background square is to be fussy-cut as described in chapter three, use the quarter-square template (Fig. 7, page 62) with the ¼" seam allowance masked off to determine yardage requirements for the four patches.

Once you have fussy-cut any patchwork, including the Mariner's Compass block, you will look at bolts of fabric in an entirely new way. You may find yourself in the middle of a quilt shop opening up the bolt to count how many repeating motifs are printed across the width. Fabrics that may not have appealed to you before because they seemed too busy or unusable may become your very favorites for fussy-cutting.

Fussy-cut Mariner's Compass ✿ Ann S. Lainhart

Drafting Mariner's Compasses

If you would like to dive right in to making a block, skip these drafting instructions. Go directly to the end of this chapter where you will find directions for preparing templates for the 12" and 18" Compasses.

Since grade school I have been using a ruler, protractor, compass, pencil, and paper to draw geometric designs. Drafting my own Mariner's Compasses came naturally to me. The idea of drafting a Compass may be intimidating to some, but my method requires little math. Every student in every Mariner's Compass workshop I have taught has accomplished it beautifully. Just follow the directions step-by-step to draw each part of the block precisely.

Most of the Mariner's Compass blocks I make are one of three sizes: a 16-point Compass with two rows of points that finishes 12" in diameter; a 32-point Compass with three rows of points that finishes 18" in diameter; or a 48-point Compass with three rows of points that finishes 30" in diameter. However, you can draft a Compass any size by following these directions and altering the measurements to fit your block.

Materials

⚙ Paper at least 2" wider than the finished Compass block

⚙ 6" diameter protractor with easy-to-see markings

⚙ Regular compass

⚙ Beam compass (see how to make one below) or a yardstick compass available from amisimms.com

⚙ Mechanical pencil or sharp pencils

⚙ Eraser

⚙ Flat ruler such as an architectural ruler—the marked edge of the ruler should be flat against the paper. Do not try to draft with a rotary ruler.

⚙ Permanent-ink pen such as Sharpie® Ultra-Fine Point

⚙ Thick template plastic with a printed grid. See Resources. Do not use the template plastic that comes in a roll.

Making a Homemade Beam Compass

To draw circles large enough for the Mariner's Compass blocks, you need an extended-arm drafting compass called a beam compass or a yardstick compass like the one shown in figure 1 that fits an Omnigrid® ruler.

You can make a similar tool with which to draft large circles. The largest circle used in these Compass blocks has a radius of 15". To make a compass that can be used for any of the three block sizes, cut a piece of poster board 1" x 18". With an ice pick, make a tiny hole centered 1" from the end of the poster board strip. From that hole, measure 6", 9", and 15" along the strip. Make a hole at each of the measurements just large enough for a pencil lead to pass through. This is your beam compass.

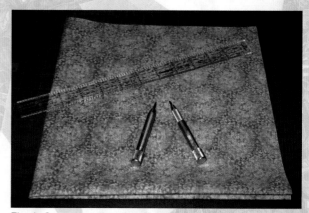

Fig. 1. Compass points that fit a ruler are useful when drawing a circle with a radius larger than 5".

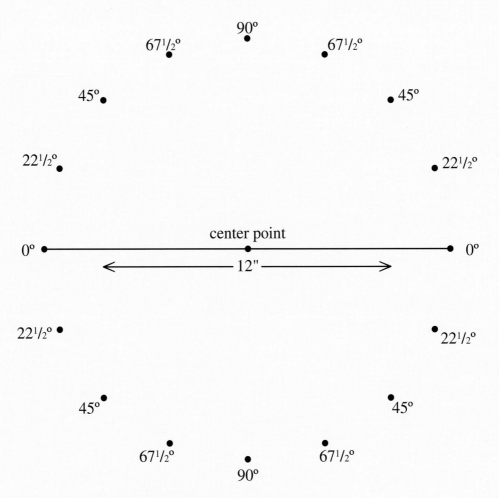

Fig. 2. A 12" line with degree marks is the starting point for drafting a 12" Compass block.

Drafting a 16-Point 12" Mariner's Compass

This block has two layers of points. The first layer in the block's center has eight points and the secondary row has eight as well. Start with a paper at least 14" square. In the center of the paper, draw a 12" horizontal line and mark the center point.

Place the protractor on the horizontal line matching the center points. Put a pencil mark at the edge of the protractor at 22½°, 45°, 67½°, 90°, 67½°, 45°, and 22½° as shown. Rotate the protractor, and mark the same degrees on the other half of the paper below the center horizontal line (Fig. 2).

Place one end of a yardstick compass or beam compass in the middle of the horizontal line, and draw a circle with a radius of 6". The circle should just touch the ends of the drawn line. If you are using the homemade cardboard compass, poke a thumbtack through the hole near the end of the strip and place it at the center point of the horizontal line. Lightly hold the strip in place with the thumbtack. Insert a pencil into the 6" hole and swing the strip around the center, drawing a circle around the line.

Align the flat ruler across the circle from one mark to the opposite mark. The edge of the ruler should pass through the center point of the horizontal line. Draw a

12" line between the marks. Repeat at all the degree marks to divide the circle with eight 12" lines (Fig. 3). Mark the ends of the 0° horizontal line, the 45° lines, and the 90° lines with a little star to identify which lines are the primary points.

With the regular compass, draw a small circle in the center (Fig. 3). The larger the circle is drawn, the wider the points are in the center; the smaller the circle, the narrower the points. I find a circle with a radius of 1¼" makes a nice size point for the 12" Compass block.

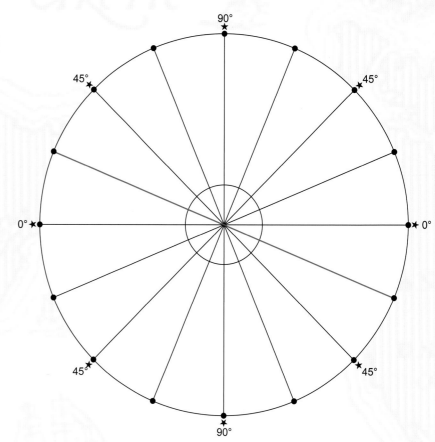

Fig. 3. Stars indicate where primary points will be. The radius of the smaller circle dictates the shape of the points.

To create the eight primary points (the points that will meet in the center), align the edge of the ruler with the end of a starred line and alongside one edge of the small center circle. Draw from the end of the line to the side of the circle, but not beyond. Line up the same end of the same line with the other side of the center circle and draw that line (Fig. 4).

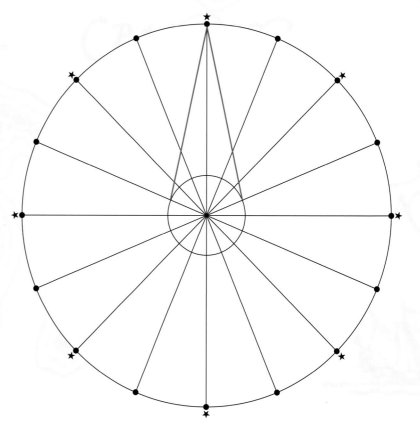

Fig. 4. Take care with precision in your drafting of the first primary point to prevent mistakes later.

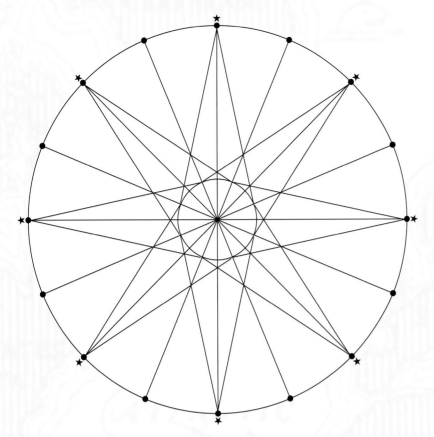

Fig. 5. All eight primary points should be exactly equidistant.

Repeat for the other seven primary points (Fig. 5). Check to see that they are equally distant from each other.

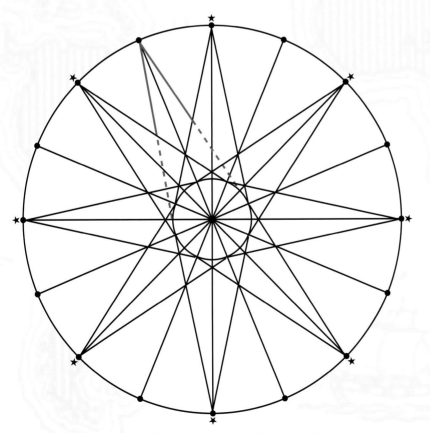

Fig. 6. Create the secondary points by drawing just to the edges of the primary points.

For the eight secondary points (the ones that lie between the primary points), align the flat ruler's edge with the end of an unstarred line and along one side of the center circle. Draw from the end of the line until you hit the primary point. Do not draw all the way to the circle. Draw the other side of this secondary point by lining up the end of the same line with the other side of the circle, stopping when you hit the primary point (Fig. 6).

Repeat with the other secondary points (Fig. 7).

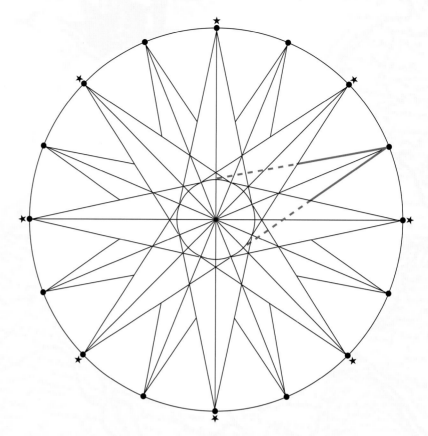

Fig. 7. All of the secondary points should be equidistant from each other and the primary points.

Erase parts of the previously drawn lines as needed to isolate the shapes for the templates. Outline one primary point, one secondary point, and one background triangle in black. Include the center lines of the patches (Fig. 8).

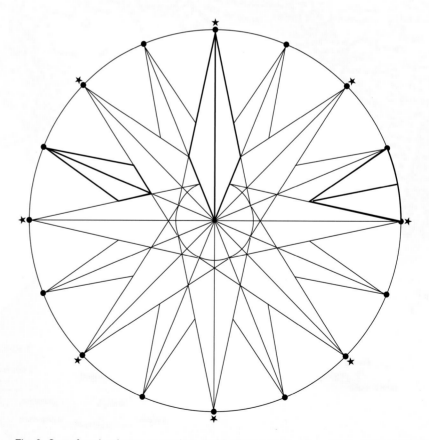

Fig. 8. One of each primary, secondary, and background triangle patch is shown outlined in heavier black lines. The center line remains on each patch for aligning templates on fabric motifs.

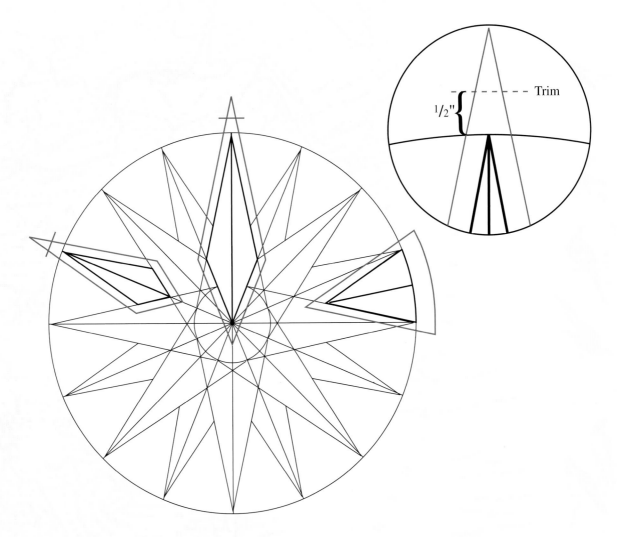

Fig. 9. One-half inch seam allowances along the outer edge of the Compass ensure sharp points for a better design result. Interior seam allowances are one-quarter inch.

Sharp points are an important design element of a pieced Compass block. A point that has a tip blunted by the background square is sure to be noticed. To ensure that the tips of points won't get cut off when the Compass is inset in the square, I add ½" seam allowances at the outer points. To do this, using the ¼" line on an acrylic ruler, add ¼" seam allowances on the straight sides of the primary and secondary points, drawing the lines until they meet past the points.

Refer to figure 9. On the primary point pattern, trim the end of the point that's at the outer edge of the circle, leaving a ½" seam allowance at the tip as shown in the detail. Repeat this on the secondary point.

Also add a ½" seam allowance along the curved edge of the background triangular patch. You can accomplish this "by eye," or use the beam compass set ½" wider to add this curved allowance.

These ½" seam allowances at the edge of the Compass make it easier to sew the block into the background square and help to produce sharp points. Look at the full-size patterns given at the end of this chapter to be sure you add the seam allowances correctly.

Drafting a 32-Point 18" Mariner's Compass

This Compass has three layers of points—eight in the center, eight in the second layer, and 16 in the third layer. Start with paper at least 20" square. In the center of the paper, draw an 18" horizontal line and mark the center point. Center the protractor on the line. On the left side of the line, place a pencil mark at the edge of the protractor at 11¼°, 22½°, 34¼°, 45°, 56¼°, 67½°, 78¼°, and 90°. Repeat on the right side of the line. Rotate the protractor and mark the same degrees below the line (Fig. 10).

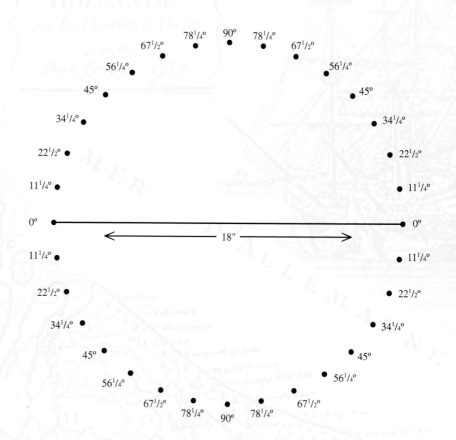

Fig. 10. Each pencil dot represents a degree mark needed for an 18" compass.

Follow directions for the 12-inch Compass to draw a circle with a 9" radius around the line. The degree marks will be on the circle. Align a flat ruler between two opposite degree marks and draw a line 18" long from one side of the circle to the opposite. The line should pass through the center of the horizontal line. Repeat to draw a total of 16 lines. Place a star at the ends of the horizontal line and at the 45° and 90° marks to indicate the primary points. Mark a plus sign at the ends of the 22½° and 67½° lines to indicate the secondary points (Fig. 11).

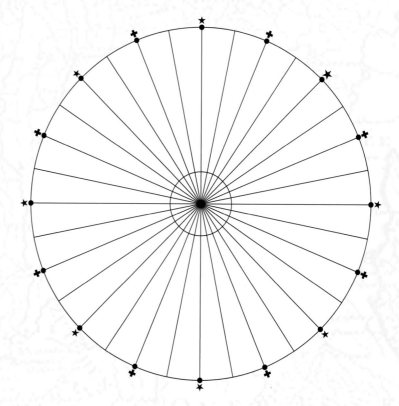

Fig. 11. Draw in all the lines. Add 8 stars and 8 plus signs as shown.

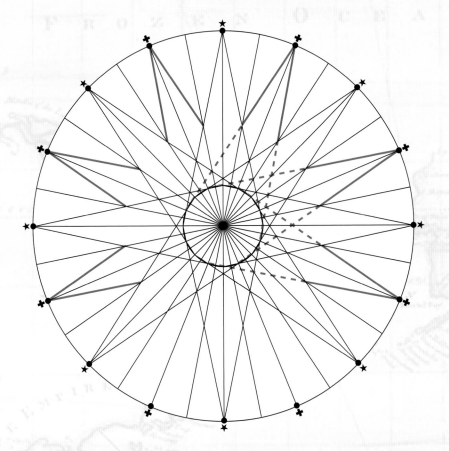

With the regular compass, draw a small circle in the center. A circle with a radius of 2" makes a nice size point for this 18" block. Check the drafting as you go to identify any mistakes.

Follow directions for the 12-inch Compass to draft the eight primary points at the lines marked with stars. Draw the eight secondary points, shown in red, at the lines marked with plus signs (Fig. 12). Not all of the secondary points are completed in the illustration.

Fig. 12. All of the primary points are shown in black. Three completed secondary points are drawn in red; three others have dashed red lines to the center circle.

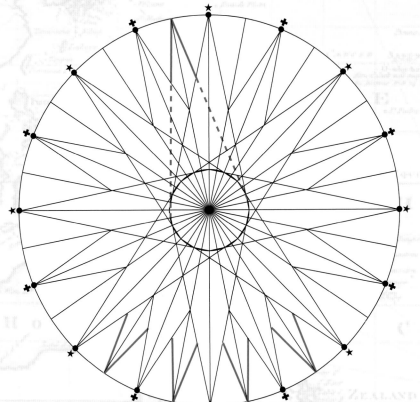

For the 16 tertiary points, line up the outside end of a remaining line with the edge of the circle on one side. Draw from the end of the line until you hit a previously drawn line. Do not draw all the way to the circle. Draw the other side of this tertiary point by lining up the outside end of the line with the other edge of the circle, drawing from the end of the line until you hit a previously drawn line (Fig. 13). Repeat to draw a total of 16 tertiary points.

Fig. 13. The tertiary points are surprisingly short as you draw them in; this is correct.

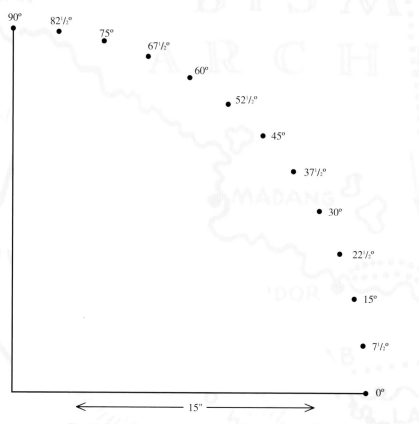

Erase some of the previously drawn lines to obtain the four patches. Outline one primary point, one secondary point, one tertiary point, and a background triangle in black (Fig. 14). Add seam allowances as described for the 12" Compass block.

Fig. 14. To best see all four types of patches, remove all drafting lines inside the patches as shown in four of them here, but leave the center lines. There is no center line in the triangle background patch.

Drafting a 48-Point 30" Mariner's Compass

This Compass has three layers of points—12 points in the center, 12 secondary points, and 24 tertiary points. For this larger Compass, draft just a quarter of it to save paper and time.

Start with paper at least 20" square. Starting about 3" from the lower left corner of the paper, draw a 15" horizontal line. Draw another 15" line at one end perpendicular to the first. Make marks along the edge of a protractor at 7½°, 15°, 22½°, 30°, 37½°, 45°, 52½°, 60°, 67½°, 75°, and 82½° as shown in figure 15.

Fig. 15. Draw two 15" perpendicular lines, and mark dots with degree labels.

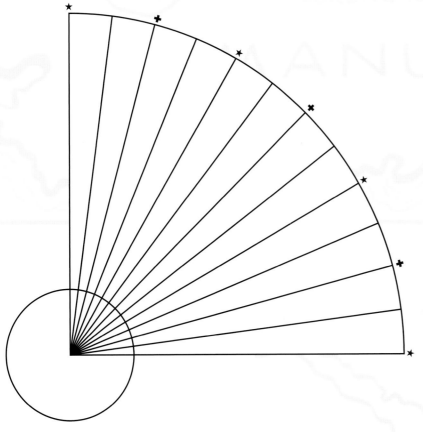

Use a beam compass to draw a quarter circle with a 15" radius. The degree marks will be inside the circle. Align a ruler with the corner and a degree mark, and draw a line 15" long. The line should touch the quarter circle. Repeat to draw a total of 11 lines. Mark the 0°, 30°, 60°, and 90° lines with a star; mark the 15°, 45°, and 75° lines with a plus sign.

Fig. 16. Use stars and plus signs to differentiate the primary and secondary points.

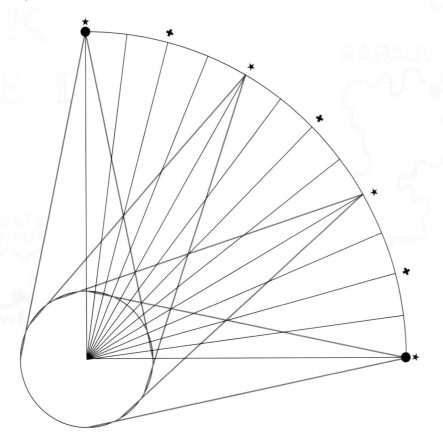

With the regular compass draw a complete small circle in the center (Fig. 16). I find a circle with a radius of 2½" makes attractive points for this 30" size Compass.

To create the center primary points, position the ruler from the outside end of any line marked with a star to the edge of the center circle on one side and draw a line. Draw from the same outside end of the line to the other side of the circle. Repeat with all lines marked with stars (Fig. 17).

Fig. 17. Mark the four primary points in this quarter.

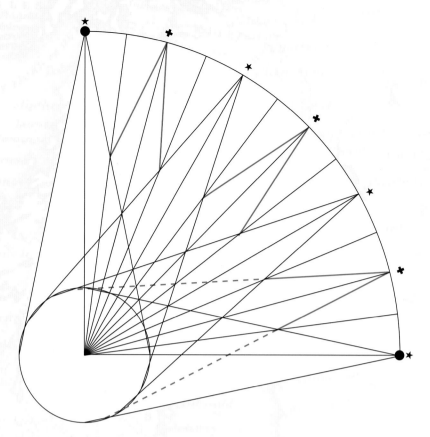

Fig. 18. Mark the secondary points.

For the secondary points, position the ruler from the outside end of a line with a plus sign with the edge of the circle on one side. Draw from the outside end of the line until you hit a previously drawn line. Do not draw all the way to the circle. Draw the other side of this secondary point in the same manner (Fig. 18). Repeat with the remaining secondary points.

For the tertiary points, line up the outside end of a remaining line with the edge of the circle on one side. Draw from the outside end of the line until you hit a previously drawn line. Draw the other side of this tertiary point in the same manner (Fig. 19). Repeat to draft the remaining points.

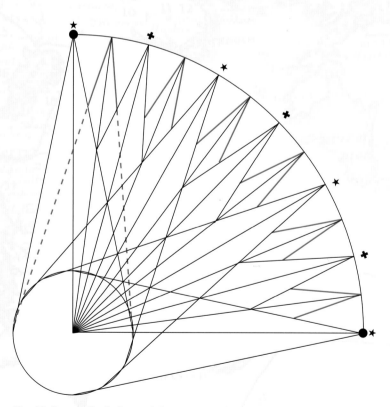

Fig. 19. Draw in the tertiary points.

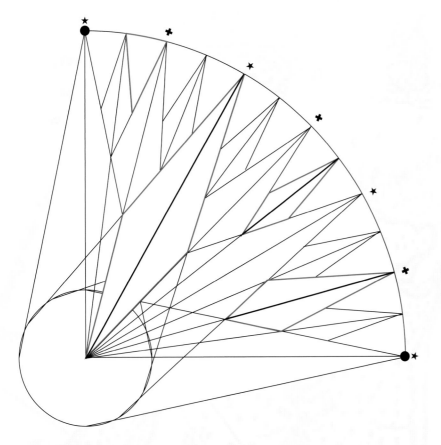

Erase parts of some of the previously drawn lines. Outline one primary point, one secondary point, one tertiary point, and a background triangle in black (Fig. 20). Add seam allowances as described for the 12" Compass block.

Fig. 20. Outline 4 patches in heavier lines, and keep the center lines in the points to use when aligning templates on fabric.

Preparing Templates

Template plastic comes in 8½" x 11" sheets and 11" x 17" sheets. If a patch is too large to fit on a sheet of the template plastic, butt 2 sheets edge to edge and tape them together on both sides. I prefer using a heavier plastic with a printed ¼" grid so that I can position a grid line through the center of each template. The thicker plastic allows each fabric patch to be cut out with a rotary cutter; the plastic is thick enough to feel its edge as you cut. If you nick it, you can always make another one.

Template patterns for the 12" and 18" Compass blocks are given on pages 38 and 39. Use these or your own drafted patterns to make a template for each patch. Trace all lines onto the plastic, including the center line in each patch. Though you can cut the templates out with scissors, trimming off the outer pen line as you cut, I prefer to cut them using a rotary cutter and rotary ruler. This gives the templates a much smoother, straight edge. Use the templates to make the Compass blocks as described in chapter three.

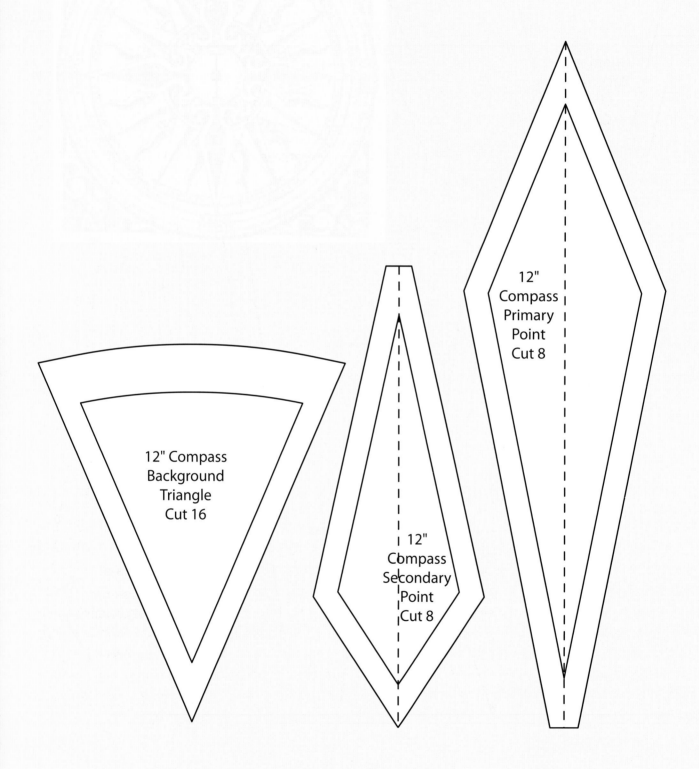

12" Compass
Background
Triangle
Cut 16

12"
Compass
Secondary
Point
Cut 8

12"
Compass
Primary
Point
Cut 8

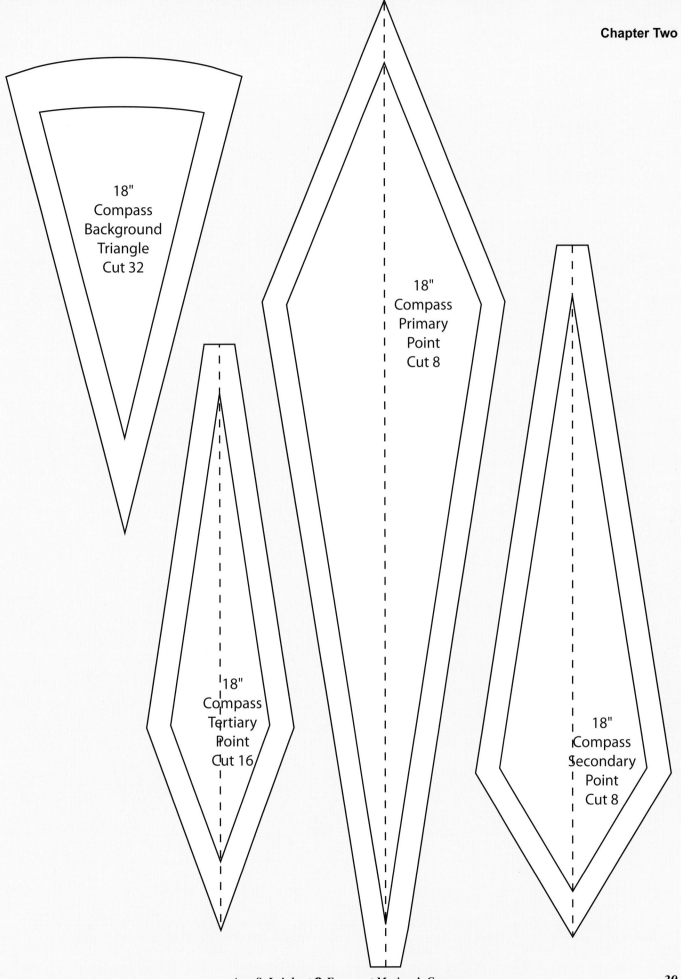

18"
Compass
Background
Triangle
Cut 32

18"
Compass
Primary
Point
Cut 8

18"
Compass
Tertiary
Point
Cut 16

18"
Compass
Secondary
Point
Cut 8

Fussy-cut Mariner's Compass ✪ *Ann S. Lainhart*

Making Pretty Mariner's Compasses

Each size of a Mariner's Compass block has a unique set of patches.
You'll find directions for drafting Compasses, templates for the
12" and 18" Compass blocks, and how to prepare templates in chapter two.

Selecting the Motifs

Once you have made the templates, then it's time to begin the most creative part of the process—choosing and fussy-cutting the specific motifs for the Mariner's Compass patches. Since the eight primary points come together for the kaleidoscopic center, they are the focal point, and thus they are the most important patches to fussy-cut.

Look for fabric design elements that flow from one patch to the next or that make a pretty pattern when joined (Fig. 1, page 43). For example, a half circle at the edge of a patch becomes a circle when two patches are sewn together.

While the design in the points that come together in the center of the Mariner's Compass is the most important element, you also must be aware of what motif appears in the long points at the outer edge of the circle.

If the fabric from which you cut the primary points has areas of the same color as the background fabric, then make sure that this color is not along the edges of the long points. Otherwise, the distinct edge of the outer points may disappear against the background.

To identify symmetrical designs that will be appropriate for the primary points, tape ¼" masking tape along the edges of the template in the seam allowances so that what you see is what you get when the patches are joined.

Fussy-cutting Tips

* Stick ¼" wide masking tape over the seam allowance of each template so that all you see when the template is on the fabric is what will be seen in the finished block.

* Trace major elements of the fabric design on the template using a Sharpie® extra fine pen. Then position the traced lines on the template in exactly the same position on the fabric each time.

* Cut only one layer of the fabric at a time to ensure that each patch is cut from the exact same motif.

* Replace the blade in your rotary cutter with a new one when you begin a new quilt, so that the patches can be cut as easily and accurately as possible.

* Place the cutting mat near a corner of a table so that you can move your body around as needed to make continuous cuts around the template.

* To prevent the yardage from falling off the table edge as you cut, place weights to hold the fabric in place.

* If the plastic template gets nicked while cutting, make a new one.

Fig. 1. The delicate circle and motifs in the primary points in this block are a result of the careful placement of the fabric's design elements.

Position the template on various parts of the fabric, rotating it at each spot. What might not work in one direction may be perfect when the template is turned upside down. The motif needs to fill the entire point in an interesting way (Fig. 2). Place a piece of masking tape on the fabric in the center of any likely design so you don't lose track of it as you search for other possibilities.

Some quiltmakers use hinged mirrors to audition possible motifs. Use two mirrors or mirrored tiles each about 4" x 6" or larger. Larger mirrors will show more of the kaleidoscope image that will be visible.

Fig. 2. Note how much goes on in the center of this Compass. Light patches surround the dark primary points, and a light inner star fills the center.

Ann S. Lainhart ✷ *Fussy-cut Mariner's Compass*

Fig. 3. The contrast between the three types of points and the background fabric is very important.

Tape the mirrors together along one edge to make a hinge. Center the plastic template for the primary point on the fabric. Position the hinged mirrors at the short end of the template ¼" in from the edges at a 45-degree angle. The pattern is repeated eight times in the mirrors just as it will look in the pieced block. Audition each potential design in this manner.

If you prefer allowing serendipity to take over, cut two primary points from a likely motif. Sew them together to see if the design produced along the seam line is pleasing. You may enjoy being surprised by this more spontaneous method.

The secondary points do not touch each other, so fussy-cutting them is easier because it is not critical that the same design appears at the edge of each patch. Simply place the plastic template on the fabric, shifting it until you locate a lovely motif. Choose an image that contrasts with the primary points (Fig. 3).

Be sure that the outer edges of the points contrast with the background triangle patches as well so the edges of the secondary points are distinct. Cut each of the patches alike.

The tertiary points in a larger Compass should contrast with the primary points, the secondary points, and the background triangle patches.

Fussy-cutting the Patches

Once you have chosen the motif, it's time to cut patches. Read the sidebar on page 42 for fussy-cutting tips.

Place the template on the fabric, making sure the center line marked on the template runs along the center of the motif.

With a permanent-ink pen, trace the major design elements on the template so every fussy-cut patch can be cut from the same position on the fabric.

Once the template is in place, it is best not to release it before the entire patch is cut out. If the template starts to shift, tape it in place on both sides.

Although the template can be drawn around with a pencil and the fabric patch cut out with scissors, I recommend against this approach for two reasons:

First, the pencil may pull on the fabric, and that can lead to distortion that makes matching the design in the center difficult.

Second, many pencils, especially light-colored ones, are soft and do not hold a sharp point, so your drawn line may be too wide. Then the question becomes where to cut—on the inside of the line, down the middle, or on the outside of the line? This can lead to cut patches that are inaccurate enough to make matching the design in the center difficult. I prefer cutting the fabric patches with a rotary cutter.

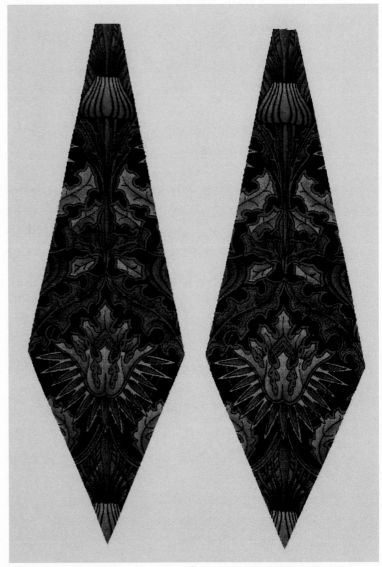

Fig. 4. Cut all primary points from the same repeat of the fabric motif.

The heavy gridded template plastic that I recommend is thick enough to feel the edge with your rotary cutter. Place the blade against the template at one end of the patch. Cut backwards for just a short distance to make sure you cut past the end of the template, and then slowly cut forward just past the end of that side, keeping the blade against the template. Repeat on all sides.

Use enough pressure to make sure you are cutting through the layer of fabric. Compare the fabric patches to be sure that the motifs are cut exactly alike (Fig. 4).

Be aware that all sides of the patches are on the bias, so as you handle and work with them, especially when pressing, they may stretch.

Each patch must be marked on the wrong side where the seams intersect so that any stretching can be eased back in as the patches are joined. These marks are important for setting in the patches.

Place a flat ruler along the edge of the wrong side of a fabric point with most of the ruler off the patch and the ¼" line along the cut edge. Mark short pencil lines at about ¼" from each end of the patch, except at the point on the long edge, where the mark should be about ½" from the end. (Fig. 5).

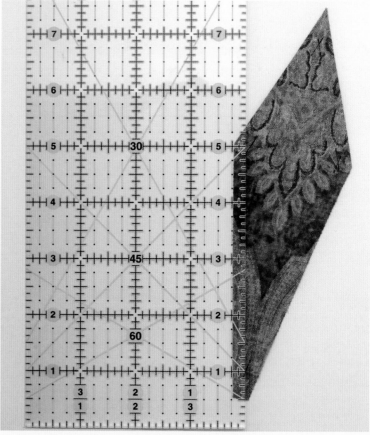

Fig. 5. Precision marking is as important as precision cutting.

Rotate the ruler along the adjacent edge and make a short mark at about ¼" from each end, except at the point on the long edge where the mark should be about ½" from the end.

Repeat with the other two sides. Marking this way results in crosses that can be matched up with crosses on the other patches.

For the triangular background patches, mark the two straight sides in the same way, but at each end of the curved edge, align the ½" line of the ruler with the cut edge of the patch, and mark ½" from the curved end. Repeat to mark all the patches (Fig. 6).

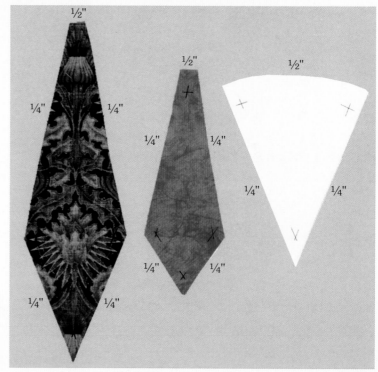

Fig. 6. Marking ½" seam allowances along the outside points and the curve of the background triangle makes it easier to obtain sharp points when the Compass is stitched into the background square.

Piecing the Block

While the kaleidoscopic center of a Compass is the focal point, sharp points at the edge of the circle are also important in a well-made block.

Place two primary point patches right sides together, matching edges and the crossed lines at the short end. Bring a pin up through the center of the crossed lines on the wrong side of one patch and through the lines on the other patch. Leave the pin dangling vertically in the patches.

Slightly pull apart the patches. Pass a pin through a portion of the motif that is ¼" from the edge of one patch, and then pass the tip of the pin through the same spot in the motif on the second patch. Again,

allow the pin to dangle in place. Continue to match and pin spots about every ½" along the edge, and pin the marked lines at the end (Fig. 7).

Bring the edges together and insert a pin through both layers beside each dangling pin, removing the dangling pins as edges are secured. Taking the time to match the motifs guarantees that the kaleidoscopic design will meet neatly after stitching.

Sew from the edge of the fabric in the center (the short point) to the crossed lines where the secondary point will be inset. Do not sew to the edge of the fabric at the end. Backstitch to secure (Fig. 8). Finger press the seam allowance to one side. Do not iron this seam. Repeat to make 4 pairs like this.

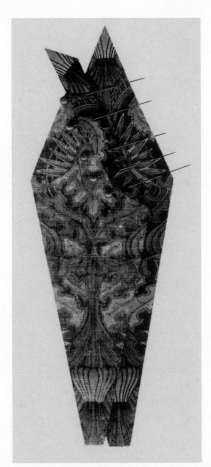

Fig. 7. In this pinned patch, the top patch is pulled back so you can see designs on both patches from the right side.

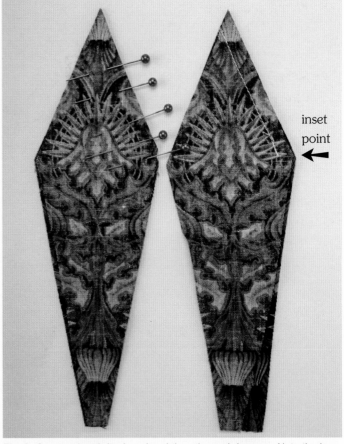

inset point

Fig. 8. One patch pair is pinned and the other pair is sewn. Note the location of the inset point.

Join two pairs to make half the block center, stopping stitches at the crossed lines at the inset points. Finger press all seam allowances in the same direction.

Repeat to make a second half in the same way, pressing the seam allowances just as you did the first half.

Pin the two halves together (Fig. 9). The seam allowances on the top half should butt into the seam allowances on the bottom half to allow them to pinwheel as described next. Sew from one inset point to the opposite inset point, back-stitching at the beginning and end of the seam.

Fig. 9. If the finger-pressed seams butt when the halves are pinned, printed motifs are easier to align properly.

Pull out the few stitches in the seam allowance in the center that are perpendicular to the final seam so that the allowances can be rotated to form a pinwheel (Fig. 10). Do not iron this seam yet. I call this pieced center the "spider" since there are eight "legs."

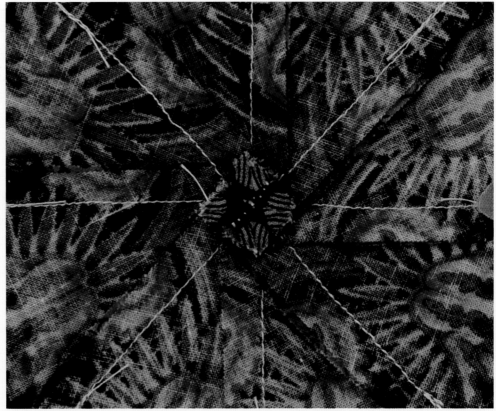

Fig. 10. Pulling 2 or 3 stitches to allow the final seam to lie flat will not harm the integrity of the block.

Turn the block over and check that all design motifs align as you wish (Fig. 11). If not, now is the time to restitch any of the patches. Set the center aside for now.

Fig. 11. Check the front of the sewn patches for design alignment.

Position a background triangle on top of a secondary point patch, matching and pinning the marks at both ends.

Sew from the edge of fabric at the wide part of the point to the edge of fabric at the wide part of the background triangle, stitching through the marks to the edge of the patches (Fig. 12).

Finger press the background patch and seam allowances away from the secondary point patch.

Line up and pin the other side of the point with a second background triangle.

Stitch again from the wide part of the point and make sure this seam crosses the previous seam at the ½" mark at the outside edge (Fig. 13). Finger press the seam allowances away from the point.

Check that the point patch is the right length. To do this, on the front side of the unit, measure from the tip of the point to the curved edge of the unit (Fig.

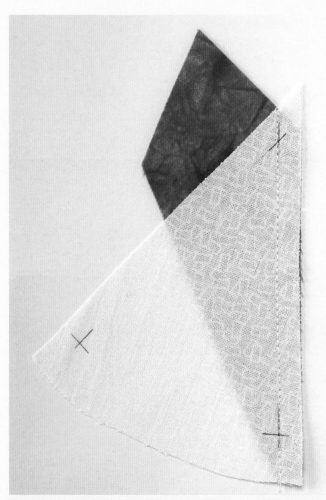

Fig. 12. The usefulness of precise marking shows on the back of this background patch/point combination.

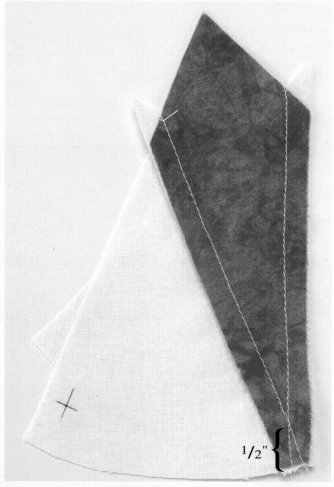

Fig. 13. The two seams should crisscross each other ½" from the edge.

14). If the length is ½" or a little more, then the point is good and won't get cut off by the fabric frame that will be added later.

If it measures less than ½" to the edge, then the frame may cut off the point. To prevent that, resew the last seam you made, taking a slightly larger seam allowance—two or three threads.

In figure 15, the white thread is the first line of stitching and the red thread is the second line of stitching. There is no reason to remove the first seam. This process shortens the point so the frame will not cut it off.

Repeat these steps to make seven more pieced units.

These pieced units are inset into the spider. With right sides together, match and pin the marks at each end of the appropriate patches. Sew from the outside edge toward the marked inset point. A

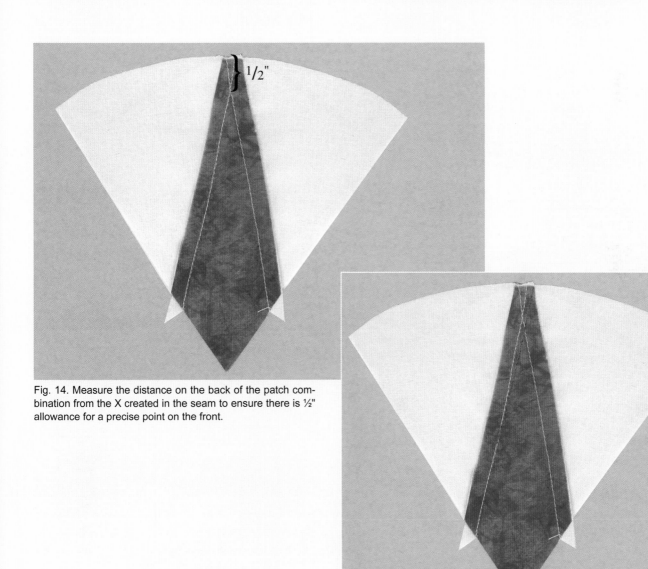

Fig. 14. Measure the distance on the back of the patch combination from the X created in the seam to ensure there is ½" allowance for a precise point on the front.

Fig. 15. Resew the second line of stitching if needed to create the ½" seam allowance at the tip.

presser foot that allows you to see the needle going into the fabric is useful.

As you approach the inset point, make sure that all seam allowances are out of the way.

Allow the pin to slide under the presser foot, and manually turn the wheel until the needle is on top of the pin. Release the presser foot to shift the fabric slightly if necessary to make sure the needle is right on top of the pin. Carefully slide the pin out and lower the needle into the same point; backstitch to secure (Fig. 16).

Readjust and pin the unit so that it is on top of the adjacent primary point, right sides together.

As before, sew from the outside of the patches to the marked inset point, making sure all seam allowances are out of the way. Backstitch at the marked point (Fig. 17).

Turn the block right side up and check that the inset is neat and there are no puckers or holes (Fig. 18, page 53). Inset the rest of the pieced units into the spider.

Fig. 16. Careful pinning and slow stitching are important to ensure precise piecing.

Fig. 17. This back view shows how the secondary point and background triangles fit between two primary points.

Fig. 18. The front view shows an inset secondary point unit.

Remember to make sure the seams cross at the marked lines ½" from the outside edges.

It's time to press the pieced Compass. From the back, press all seam allowances away from the outer points without ironing all the way to the center.

At each inset point, three seams come together. Each has already been finger pressed in a certain direction. The seam allowances along the points are pressed away from the points, and the center seam allowances are pressed in a pinwheel.

Where the seams come together at each inset point, allow the seams to overlap or fold in on themselves naturally. Finally, press the pinwheel flat in the center (Fig. 19).

Fig. 19. Press carefully to avoid stretching any bias edges.

Fig. 20. Puckers on the front side indicate a need to resew a seam.

Check from the front to be sure there are no puckers (Fig. 20).

Larger Compasses with secondary and tertiary points are pieced in much the same way. First, piece the central spider with the eight primary points.

Second, sew background triangles to each side of a tertiary point. Repeat with the other tertiary points to make 16 units like the one shown in figure 21.

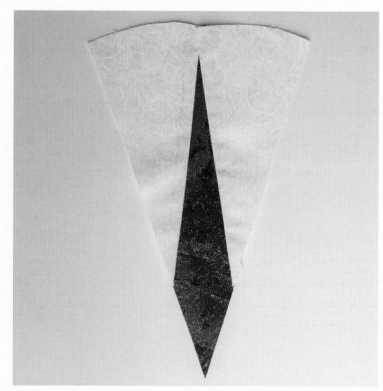

Fig. 21. Use the same techniques as before to create tertiary points.

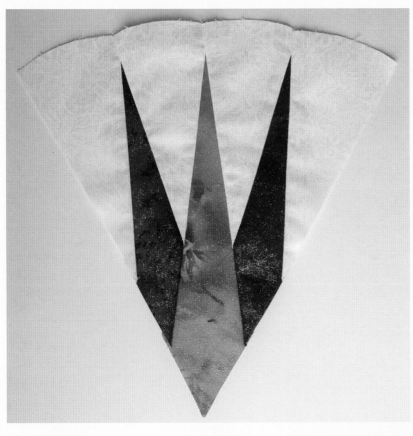

Fig. 22. The tertiary point units sewn to secondary points will be inset into the spider of primary points.

Third, sew a tertiary point unit to each side of a secondary point (Fig. 22). Repeat with the other secondary points.

Fourth, inset these pieced units into the primary-point spider to complete the Compass (Fig. 23).

Taking the time to carefully cut, mark, and pin pays off in the end with a carefully constructed fussy-cut Mariner's Compass. You'll complete the block in chapter four.

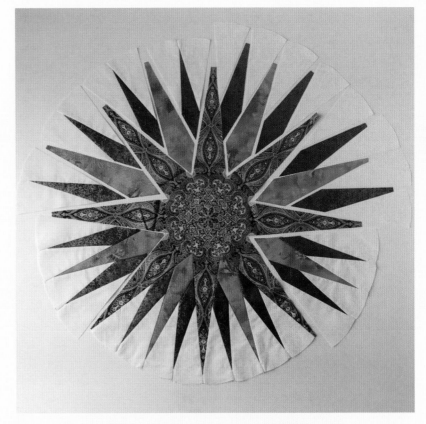

Fig. 23. This view shows the entire block from the front, with some parts left unsewn.

Fussy-cut Mariner's Compass ✿ Ann S. Lainhart

Finishing Mariner's Compass Blocks

Once the round Mariner's Compass block is made as described in chapter three, it is stitched into a background square to be used in a quilt or as a wallhanging. Here is a method that students in my workshops find easy. For ideas on how to display your blocks, see chapter five.

Cut the background square any size you wish, depending on the final use of the block. I have found that squares cut 4" larger than the Compass are in good proportion. A Mariner's Compass with a 12" diameter looks lovely in a 16" square; 18" Compasses fit into 22" squares; and 30" Compasses look best in 34" or 36" squares.

Cutting the Background Square

Audition the background fabric once the pieced Compass is made, if you haven't already chosen it. You may be surprised how different background fabrics will bring out certain colors in the Compass patches. What looks ordinary on a light fabric might pop and look amazing on a dark print, or vice versa.

Select a fabric that will enhance the colors in the Compass, not overpower them. Try different types and scales of prints. If the Compass patches have a lot of pattern, you may prefer a more subdued, less busy print for the frame. For example, tone-on-tone prints look like a mat surrounding the Compass.

With my method, a circle is cut from the center of the background square, and the Mariner's Compass is stitched into the center by machine. The cut circle has a radius that is ½" less than the radius of the finished size of the Compass. For a 12" Compass with a 6" radius, the radius of the circle cut from the 16" square is 5½". For an 18" Compass, the cut circle has a radius of 8½". For a 30" Compass, the cut circle has a radius of 14½".

The samples that follow are for an 18" Mariner's Compass. Fold the 22" background square into quarters. A regular compass for drafting circles will not open wide enough to mark the circle needed. I suggest using a beam compass or yardstick compass, or make your own out of poster board as described in chapter two.

On the folded fabric square, draw a quarter circle with a radius of 8½" (Fig. 1). With a rotary cutter, fitted with a new blade for a sharp, clean cut, slowly cut out this quarter circle along the marked line, making sure you are cutting through all four layers of fabric at once. Do not lift the rotary cutter from the fabric until you've completed the entire cut. If the fabric gets pushed ahead by the rotary cutter, stop without removing the cutter from the fabric and smooth the fabric flat again.

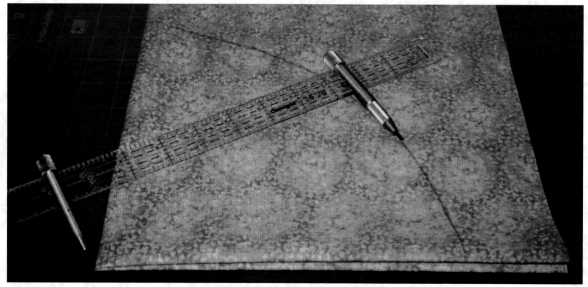

Fig. 1. Use the compass points to draw a quarter circle. Change your rotary blade so you can cut smoothly through all four fabric layers without distorting the fabric.

Setting the Compass into the Background

With matching thread, sew a line of stay-stitching a scant ½" from the edge of the background circle with a matching thread—that is, stitch a couple of threads narrower than ½". (The illustration uses a dark thread so it is visible.)

Refold the square into quarters, and mark the four fold points with pins at the edge of the circle. These will align with the four primary points of the Compass.

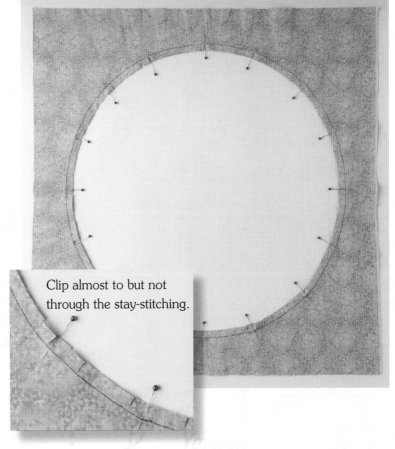

Clip almost to but not through the stay-stitching.

Fig. 2. Staystitching requires a slow, steady pace and gentle handling to prevent stretching or distorting the fabric.

Fold the background square pin to pin to mark four more primary points. Fold the space between these pins to mark the eight secondary points.

Clip about every ½" around the circle almost to the staystitching but not through it and not where there is a pin (Fig. 2).

Lay the Compass right side up and place the square right side up on top of it. Line up the primary points correctly with the square (Fig. 3).

Fig. 3. Help maintain accuracy by being sure the primary points are north, south, east, and west. This is easier on your eyes.

Fig. 4. Use the dangling pin method of pinning described in chapter three to ensure accuracy.

Fold the square down over the Compass with right sides together, aligning the marking pins with the north, south, east, and west primary points. Pin the framing square to the Compass in those four places (Fig. 4).

Fig. 5. You may feel as if you are overpinning, but this technique yields the best results.

In the same manner, pin the remaining primary and secondary points. Make sure the raw edge of the Compass and the cut edge of the circle match.

Pin between the first pins so that the Compass is securely set into the square (Fig. 5).

Fig. 6. Because very few people examine finished quilts or framed blocks up close, and because the overall visual impact of the block will be affected by the sharpness of your points, a little variation at the tips will go unnoticed, so long as they are, indeed, sharp.

With thread that matches the square, stitch just to the left, inside the row of staystitching. Remove pins as you come to them.

Open up the square and iron it away from the Mariner's Compass so the seam allowances are under the square. If any of the staystitches are visible, remove them with a pin or restitch that section of the circle. If you wish, trim the seam allowance to ¼".

It's okay if all the points do not touch the circle in precisely the same way. That is much less noticeable than points that are cut off by the frame (Fig. 6).

Making a Fussy-cut Background

Several of the 18" Compasses shown in the book have background squares made from four fussy-cut pieces rather than one single square. This fussy-cutting can be done with the same fabric used in any of the pieced points or with a totally different fabric.

To make a pattern for a fussy-cut background square for any size Mariner's Compass, divide the measurement of the background square in half, and draw a square that size on paper. For an 18" Compass with a 22" background square, draw an 11" square.

From one corner of the square, draw a quarter circle with a radius that is ½" smaller than the radius of the finished Compass block. In this case, the 18" Compass has a radius of 9", so draw a quarter circle with a radius of 8½".

Add ¼" seam allowance to the two short ends as shown in figure 7. Fold the paper in half and mark the midpoint of the curve. Draw a line from the midpoint to the corner of the square. This

Fig. 7. Use only a ¼" seam allowance for ends of the background square.

line will be used to align the template on the fabric motif for fussy-cutting.

Transfer the paper pattern to template plastic. Since you can see through the plastic, it is easier to fussy-cut the four corner frames all alike. Use a heavy template plastic that you can cut around with a rotary cutter when cutting fabric patches. If needed, tape pieces of plastic together along their edges to make a larger template. Transfer the lines from the paper pattern to the template plastic, including the center line.

Cut the template out using a rotary cutter and ruler if you can to obtain a smooth line. If that seems too difficult, cut it out with scissors, trimming off the outer drawn lines.

Place the template on the fabric with the center line through the middle of the symmetrical motif. For the design to be the same at both short ends, the center drawn line may need to be aligned with the straight grain of the fabric. If that's the case, the outer edges of the template are aligned with the bias of the fabric. That is acceptable, since in this case, the design is the most important consideration.

Use a permanent ink pen to trace the major elements of the motif onto the template. If it is difficult to hold the template in place, tape it to the fabric in several places.

Cut around the template slowly with a rotary cutter, never lifting the cutter off the fabric. Shift your body as needed to cut all the sides. Cut right through the tape. Handle the cut patch as little as possible since there are bias edges (Fig. 8).

Fig. 8. If fussy-cutting the background square patches, for best results, do not layer the fabric.

sew
together

Fig. 9. Audition the Compass and background square patches to be sure the overall design is as desired.

Position the template on a repeat of the same design, arranging the marked lines with the motif. In order to ensure that the motif aligns the same as the first patch, the fabric may have to be pulled slightly when positioning the template for cutting. Tape the template in place and cut out the fabric patch. Cut the four framing patches all alike (Fig. 9).

Sew the seams of the short edges together to make a square. Proceed as explained on the previous pages to set the Compass into the background square. Make sure you line up the north, south, east, and west points of the Compass with the seams of the background square. Once it is pressed, your Compass block is pieced and ready to use.

Displaying Mariner's Compasses

Once you have pieced one or more Mariner's Compasses, it's time to display
your handiwork. Because of the visual complexity of the Compass,
one block is all you need to make a lovely wallhanging.

Fig. 1. Nothing else is needed to enhance the beauty of a single, fussy-cut, precisely sewn Mariner's Compass block.

Fig. 2. Taped ends allow you to split the cord for an instant "hook" for the rod end.

Layer, quilt, and bind the block as you would any quilt top. A stiffer than usual filler in place of batting, such as Pellon® fleece, will keep the Compass flat against the wall. In figure 1, the same print was used for the secondary points and the background square. A solid dark binding was added to frame it.

Hang It All

One easy way to hang a small quilt is to insert a dowel or slat through the sleeve on the back of the quilt. The sleeve should end about an inch from each side of the quilt, and the dowel or slat should be cut just a little shorter than the quilt's width.

Cut a length of commercially available cord that is about 8" to 10" longer than the quilt's width. Wrap 1" at each end of the cord with tape so the ends will not untwist.

Pull the cording apart just above the tape and slide the split cord over the dowel or slat as shown in figure 2. The taped ends of the cord should be hidden underneath the edges of the quilt. Hang the cord over a hook on the wall (Fig. 3).

Fig. 3. A Mariner's Compass block is hung by a simple cord and tape system.

Fig. 4. Today's fabric lines offer a myriad of opportunities to use multiple fabrics together for one great effect.

Head for the Border

Adding a printed border stripe around the block finishes it nicely. Choose a coordinating border print cut to a width that shows the print to best advantage.

Be sure to cut the four border strips from the same part of the fabric so the identical part of the print meets in each corner, thus making another fussy-cut design on the quilt.

Sew strips around the block and miter the corners. Bind the quilt with the same or contrasting fabric.

In this 30" Mariner's Compass with 48 points, a bold, large-scale print is used in the 12 primary points. Two tone-on-tone prints are cut for the other sets of points. A small-scale print from the same fabric line used for the primary points works well for the background square, and a border print in the same line is a natural choice for the outer edges. By choosing one fabric line that has a varied range of print type and scale, you are bound to come up with a winning combination (Figs. 4–7).

Fig. 5. The large motif used in the primary points of the block in figure 4 is shown here.

Fig. 6. A small-scale coordinating fabric makes a lovely background square.

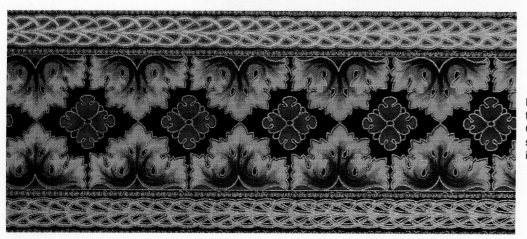

Fig. 7. A border print can be used to good effect both within the Compass points or as a border stripe to frame the block as done in the block in figure 4.

Matted and Framed

The 12" Mariner's Compasses look really great if they are simply matted instead of being inset into fabric squares. Some of the smaller Compasses in chapter one are finished this way.

Take the block to a frame shop and audition various colors of mat board. Ask a frame shop to cut a 12" circle out of the center of a 16" square of the chosen mat. Also have a 16" square of foam core cut to place behind the block.

Note that the following matting method is not archival and should not be used for antique quilt blocks.

Draw lines 8" from the foam core edges, and spray or coat the foam with repositional adhesive following the manufacturer's directions. (Fig. 8).

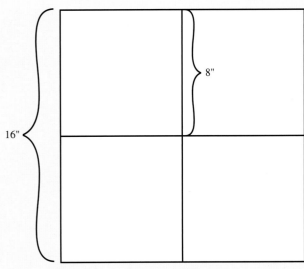

Fig. 8. Prepare the foam core to receive the Compass block.

Insert a pin through the center of the Compass and stick it into the foam core where the lines intersect. Line up the north, south, east, and west points of the Compass with the lines on the foam core.

Slowly smooth the Compass from the center out to the edges to make sure it is flat and fully attached to the foam core.

Position the mat on top of the Compass and keep it in place with double-sided tape. Insert the block in a purchased frame, with or without glass (Fig. 9).

Fig. 9. A matted Compass block can be stunning without background square fabric.

Ann S. Lainhart ✪ *Fussy-cut Mariner's Compass*

Mariner's Compasses that are inset into a fabric square can be mounted onto foam core as described above. These do not need to be matted but are simply framed, as shown in figure 10.

Fig. 10. Plan the fabric in the background square to continue design elements used in the Compass points.

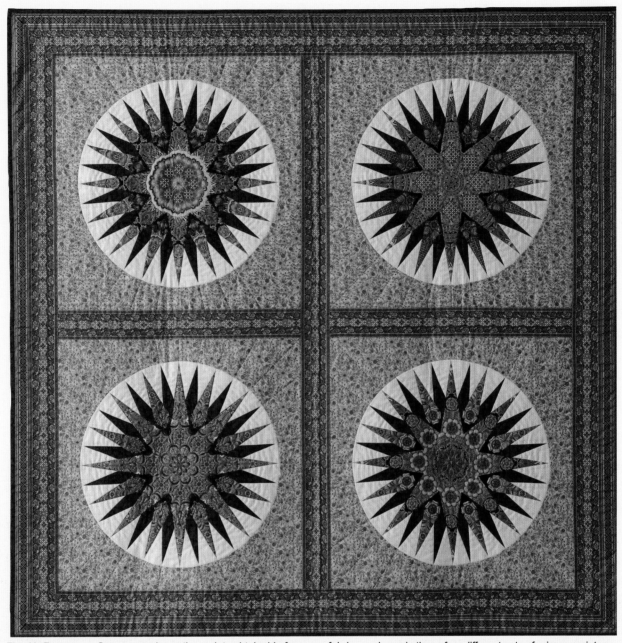

Fig. 11. FLORENTINE COMPASSES shows the variety obtainable from one fabric, as shown in these four different sets of primary points.

The More the Merrier

A larger quilt can be made by combining a sampler of Compass blocks in which the patches are fussy-cut in various ways. In FLORENTINE COMPASSES (Fig. 11), the four blocks are made with prints from the Florentine fabric line from Robert Kaufman Fabrics.

The primary points are cut from one fabric with each of the four sets cut from a different place on the print.

The secondary points, the dark blue tertiary points, the background squares, and the border and sashes are from other fabrics from the same line (Figs. 12–13, page 72).

Each block is uniquely designed so that the fussy-cut patches display the versatility of the prints. The widths of the border and sashing in quilts like this are determined by the border print motif.

Fig. 12. The primary points for FLORENTINE COMPASSES were made with this fabric.

Fig. 13. The secondary points for FLORENTINE COMPASSES were made with this fabric.

These digitally designed quilts show but a few possibilities for using fussy-cut Mariner's Compass blocks together.

In a straight vertical set as shown in figure 14, three blocks of equal size can be sewn together without sashing or setting triangles. The photo-enhanced shadow on two sides gives you a hint of what would happen if a narrow inner border or piping were added.

To construct such a quilt, join the three blocks, and add borders in widths that showcase the prints.

A quilt this lightweight can be mounted on foam core or finished as a wall quilt and hung using a rod pocket and dowel.

Fig. 14.

Fig. 15.

The intriguing design in figure 15 is a simple Nine-Patch creation displayed on point. Sew the Compass blocks alternating with plain blocks in three rows; sew the rows together. The plain blocks and corner triangles are canvasses for elegant quilting designs.

If these are finished 16" blocks, then the corner triangles can be cut as follows: Cut two squares 34⅞"

each. Cut one square on the diagonal to make two triangles. Repeat with the other square. Sew the triangles to the quilt center. This makes the outer edges of the quilt on the straight of grain.

The very simple, thin outer border is beautifully framed by a narrow binding. This quilt would also look great in a traditional picture frame.

Fig. 16.

Figure 16 shows another way to set five Compass blocks. If the blocks finish 16" square, then the four corner triangles are cut from two 12¼" squares cut once on the diagonal. The four side-setting triangles are cut from a 23⅞" square cut in half diagonally twice. This makes the outside edge of the quilt on the straight of grain.

To construct the top, sew a side-setting triangle to opposite sides of a Compass block for row 1. Join

three Compass blocks together for row 2. Make row 3 as you made row 1. Join the three rows, matching block corners carefully. Sew a corner triangle to each corner.

These setting triangles and corner squares provide great opportunities to show off quilting designs that complement the Mariner's Compass either by echoing the motifs or the points.

Random Placement

Round Mariner's Compasses of different sizes can be inset somewhat randomly into a large piece of fabric that is the same fabric used in the triangles between the points.

MORNING HAS BROKEN LIKE THE FIRST DAY, shown in figure 18, has a fussy-cut Compass inset into the lower right hand corner. The 3", 4", and 5" Compasses that represent the stars are not fussy-cut, but they show how different sizes of round blocks can be inset into a large piece of fabric.

To inset a round Compass into any background, mark where you want the center of the Compass. On the background, draw a circle with a radius ½" less than the finished radius of the Compass.

For instance, a Compass that finishes 12" in diameter has a radius of 6", so draw a circle on the background with a 5½" radius. Cut the circle on the drawn line, staystitch a scant ½" from the cut edge, clip around the circle, and inset the Compass as described in chapter four.

Fig. 17. MORNING HAS BROKEN LIKE THE FIRST DAY. The possibilities of using fussy-cut Mariner's Compass blocks are as endless as your imagination.

Fig. 18. SKY'S THE LIMIT digitally designed quilt features Sun and Star blocks.

Varying the colors as in figure 18 takes the Compass block right into the sky as a fussy-cut Sun or Star block. This digital quilt could be constructed in several ways, including setting in blocks with random placement or with fused appliqué. Once you've learned how to draft a Mariner's Compass block and mastered the fussy-cut technique, the sky truly is the limit.

As with all patchwork, don't forget to put a label on the back of your quilt that includes information about who you are and when and where the quilt was made.

Just for fun, use the fussy-cut print as the backing or the sleeve so that later you and others can see what the fabric looked like before fussy-cutting.

Resources

Template plastic may be ordered from Shoppers Rule at www.shoppersrule.com.

Design mirrors are available at quilt shops and from www.createforless.com.

Beam compasses are available from office supply stores and from www.misterart.com.

Yardstick compasses are available at quilt shops and from www.amisimms.com.

About the Author

Ann S. Lainhart

I consider myself a contemporary traditionalist when it comes to quilting. By this I mean that much of my work is based on traditional quilt blocks such as Card Trick, Mariner's Compass, and Eight-Pointed Star. But by using hand-dyed fabrics, border prints, and fussy-cutting, my quilts have a somewhat contemporary feel.

I have been quilting for more than 30 years and teaching for more than 25 years. While living in Boston, I was a member of the Proper Bostonian Quilters. When I moved to Peabody, Massachusetts, I joined the Common Threads Quilt Guild in Topsfield, Massachusetts. Currently I am a member of the East Coast Quilters Alliance and the American Quilter's Society. I also belong to the Plymouth Guild for the Arts, and my wallhangings are in the guild's galleries.

My quilts have been displayed in the Vermont Quilt Festival (a third place ribbon); the New England Images shows; and the East Coast Quilters Alliance —"A Quilter's Gathering" (I won a blue ribbon on a bargello jacket in 1998 and a white ribbon for hand quilting in 2001.)

I enjoy working with people to make commissioned wallhangings that fit their space and color scheme. I also present slide shows, trunk shows, and workshops to quilt guilds and other groups.

Please visit my Web site, which includes contact information:

The Quilted Gallery
www.quiltedgallery.com

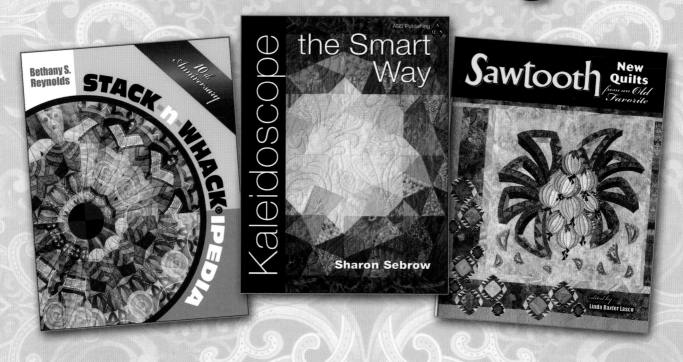